Mississippi Poems

ISBN: 978-0-9827115-2-1

A number of these poems first saw daylight in
Washing the Stones, Ibbetson Street Press, others
have been newly revised for this book, *Mississippi Poems*.

ISCSpress

Distributed by
ISCSPress
145 Foster St.
Littleton MA 01460

www.iscspress.com

Designed by Steve Glines
text: 11 pt. Garamond
titles: 22 pt. Bodoni Poster Compressed

Dedication

For Charlotte Tannheimer, a
beloved teacher, a woman of
letters, a lifelong advocate for
social justice and a delightful
friend

"Don't be afraid to tell the truth, even if it's a lie."
--Lucie Brock-Broido

Acknowledgements

I would like to thank Bill Buffett whose writing and work ethic never fail to inspire

Mark Orton and Karen Davis for teaching me the necessities of computer skills and providing valuable insight into my work

Lauren Byrne, Marc Goldfinger and Kevin McClellan for their contributions in editing my poems

Doug Holder and the Bagelbards for keeping me in the loop

Irene Koronas for supporting my aspirations

My teacher, David Semanki, for his infallible kindness and patient tutelage in the crafting of many of the poems that make up this collection

And for their ongoing love and support in good times and in bad,

The Tannheimer Family

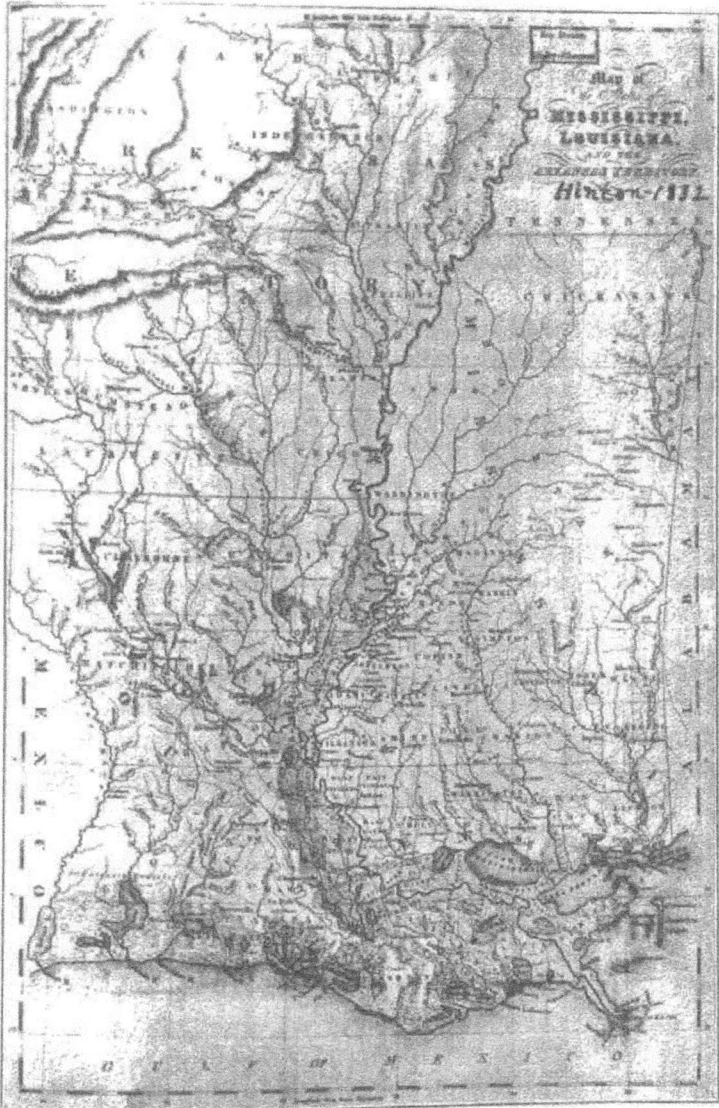

MAP OF MISSISSIPPI, 1832

Contents

MISSISSIPPI

Mississippi Poems

By Linda Larson

Sweet Dixieland, Early Sixties

I do not recall
any fine summer evening
at Jewel and Mae's
without a spreading of
the daily paper
on the picnic tables.

We cousins, second cousins
and poor neighbor
children were heaven-deep
in flushed, icy pink clots of melon
with our elbows parked
on the soaked-through newsprint,
appearing in rows of black ink
on our forearms as bits of
wet, rosy sugar punctuated by
slanted black seeds dripped
from our chins, our fingers raw
with cold, as we lazily
spit the seeds across the table
at one another until ordered to
quit it.

The aunts neatly folded up
the newspapers with their wet,
sticky contents and before our baths
we fed the watermelon rinds to the horses.

In the moonlight, our faces white as milk,
we were corralled by heat lightning
and distant thunder
onto taut, crisp, cool sheets
where we were forever safe and
even nightmares dare not intrude.

Years later I was to learn
what was written
in the newspapers
wet with melon,
discarded and forgotten
in the coming darkness.

Tornado Alley

Even over the air conditioning
she could hear the sirens sounding
in Pickens two miles away.
The keening brought her out of the double-wide,
wiping her wet hands on a tea towel.

The sky was slowly moving.
It picked up speed as
it turned from purple
corrugated thunderheads…
turned livid, the whole sky bruised,
black and blue becoming the same eerie green
as the marks he left on her arms and legs
did as they healed and in the end
even yellow before the colors petered out,
not put there by a wasted beating only
by necessity.

She had her arms and legs covered for a reason.
She had made him out a fool for the last time,
he has promised her that much and
Father and Mother on the next
much larger farm over had no pity for her.
They want this hoped-for child as much or more than
he does and who knows if they hear
her nightly screaming?
Whatever they hear she has it coming.

She had leapt from the truck and
run down Airport Road
where the crop dusters refuel and
he caught up with her on the tarmac.
She not caring if she lived or died,
begging for a ride to Kansas City,
to anywhere else…
He had popped one eardrum.
Washing his hands later,
he said she never listened to a word
he said anyway and now she had
a long white nerve dangling
where her front tooth had been
so perfect and pretty up till then.

The tornado held its breath for one instant
and her grief rose to meet it and
it was an awful thing but no
worse than he was when he
walked in the door from work,
late from work, drunk
each and every night, the only
way he could stand it himself.
Slamming the door behind him,
cornering her,
prying off his boots toe to heel,
yanking off his jeans, grabbing her
in one practiced move by the throat,
slinging her as he used to sling
calves in the junior rodeos,
when they were in high school.

By God, you will get with child--
600 acres, my ass, you will conceive
if I have to hire someone to knock you up.

And his hands would tighten on her throat
until she couldn't breathe at all
and she would stop her screams
and stop fighting him
with her arms and legs.

She had loved him, in high school,
he with the great, consoling hands.
She had loved him and his hands,
before she understood that to him
she was the land.
And the tornado came for her
and at the last it seemed
to her that he was kind.
But the storm was too great
and it, too, took her
without asking.

Dixie, 1960

As I undo your saddle belt,
you heave with relief.
When I lift it off
the leather groans and underneath
your coat is gray with sweat.
Brushing against the grain dries it off.
Careful not to startle you
into kicking the bejesus out of me,
I pat your hindquarters before moving
behind you to brush out your tail.
It is hot and bottle green horseflies
lunch on you. I slap them dead.
Blood smears where they drop
off your coat.
I loosen your bridle, and pull it off,
drinking in your wet horse smell,
while you greedily
lower your head into the water barrel,
then nudge me for more,
dripping light green water scum
onto my seersucker summer shirt.
I count to ten; you drink again.
Sweet feed: corn, oats and molasses,
two bright red Folgers coffee cans full.
In the midst of comforting sounds,
smells and stickiness, we lean soft
against each other, friends for now.
After supper,
I bring you corn shucks and watermelon rinds,
hold sugar lumps in my flattened palm.
Statues we, still dazed from the afternoon heat,
barely breathing, welcoming the coming dusk,
the pinpricks, the canopy of stars.

The Story of My Life

My mother was a knife thrower
at the carnival. I was her target
in the act. She never missed,
although I knew that sometimes
she would have liked to.

Snow Moon

A February love affair, a valentine,
a whimsy of cupid's arrow,
a flash, a falling star, a fling.
No more than that.

Your magnetism, it turned out, was
a force to be reckoned with.
North Star to my compass,
to my drifts of sand, snow,
my dreaming over decades.
All you asked of me--
allow myself to be loved.
I never thought with you around,
I would have to be the brave one.

In the mornings, swiftly, seriously,
we tend to the hole in your side
left by the tube you pulled out
without ceremony.
The piece of white plastic
put there to drain blood and
fluids from your lungs;
you declining to take your chances
of dying in a hospital, connected to all
manner of machines.

In the afternoon I lighten up,
while you with the midnight eyes,
you, who introduced me to smoke trees
and canoes, you, who saw to it
we danced our nights away
until daylight captured us,
when we would shower, rough up the dog,
then go to work fortified with a Morning Call
café au lait and a beignet.
That same you, in possession of the whole history of my happiness,
toke up deep in the afternoon, and sing along with the radio
"I want to get lost in your rock and roll and drift away."
The high from the marijuana chases away your nausea.
I read you the news; we do the jumble out loud with half a heart as
you scrutinize the hummingbirds aflame outside the picture window,
you curled up under a blanket, shivering in the heat.

The Magnolia State

White men are all right,
until they buy they're white.
Ramrod trunk, dark bark,
homely buds sprout rust-colored hairs,
blossom solitary at the end of a twig,
like a girl alone in a puddle of cream.
Magnolia, sometimes I wish they'd
buried you along with the silver.

O O O Magnolia, du wop,
God made you so simple I could eat
a magnolia sandwich and
not want another bite
all night.

I find you replete with that sassy perfume
that declares there is a difference
between the haves and the have-nots
other than having and not having.
I'd like to crinkle your petals up in my fists
and feel you bleed milk in my hands.
You are fat, sleepy, bovine
helpless flowers of the Man
and I like to eat you up.
Du wop.

Mom O Mom O Mom O Mom

Measles weren't so bad.
You running up and down
the stairs from the beauty shop,
wooing me to get better with ice cold
Coca-cola on the rocks
and a straw, one sip at a time.
White cotton gloves covered up
the angry spots on my hands.
We played twenty questions in the
evening. The doctor had said no reading.
It was like a party and I was the guest du jour.

My green parakeet, Pete,
flew out the screen door.
My sobbing hurt my throat.
You went way out on a limb,
promised me you would find him.
Later, you returned
carrying a little paper carton,
the kind chop suey comes in.
You sat beside me on the couch
and let me feel him fluttering inside.
I could almost feel his heart beating.
You told me he had been perched outside,
in the cold, clinging to the window of the pet store
right downstairs, next to the beauty shop.
I believed you.

You could be quite a spectacle yourself
when you slipped into a gala outfit with a pin
on your lapel that scraped my cheek (just a bit),
a sparkle of red across your mouth,
Revlon Fire and Ice.
You, posture perfect, three-inch heels taller,
towering over my bed, fragrant with bourbon,
cigarette smoke and Tabu. I couldn't
let this apparition disappear. I howled
when you tried to loosen my arms.
You couldn't let me go either, began
to howl yourself. Dad disentangled us
before your platinum meringue of a beehive
came all to pieces.

I Must Have Been Ten

I walked past the dazzling white sheets snapping
on the clothesline under the perfect blue sky,
laid my books on the kitchen table,
told my mother straight up,
I was finally in on the joke,
flashing her a bright and breezy smile and stealing
one of the boiled shrimp she was peeling,
There is no Jesus Christ.

Her head jerked back in surprise.
The slap had shocked us both.
She stood looking at her hand, her mouth open,
then held me close against her apron,
rife with black-eyed Susans,
briny with shrimp, her voice atremble with tears.
Told me a story about a joyride at sixteen,
an unkind stepfather, a beating, buckle-side out,
a ripped blouse, the family lined up as witnesses,
her vow to never hit a child of her own.
The promise broken to the Jesus I had already
figured out on my own didn't exist and now
it seemed I had the proof.

I pushed her away, snatched the clothespin bag,
went out the screen door to take in the sheets.

Mother's Favorite, May Day, 1959

Crayola colors, worn down to the nub,
paper peeled back, stored in the back of the closet,
replaced by the brash white mystery of training bras.

Twelve, first kiss, parakeet peck, wide-eyed,
budding in May, candy-dyed, bell-shaped
poodle skirts, taunting petticoats
the color of snow, tilted up, aglow,
pressed against the walkway,
caught in a glory moment,
safety in numbers, surrounded by sisters.

Mother's passion for azaleas,
my mother's only flaw,
her stodgy in-laws whispered
within earshot, was shared by
these rampant flowers.
"A lacking in solemnity."
Like Ma`ma, they flaunt
their imperfections, lavishly freckled
with tiny, limp antennas
only a honeybee could love.

Baby fine hair so hopelessly tangled,
it would take Tame, a hairdresser's Crisco,
before she could pull a comb through it.
I had to have the wind in my face.

Still, it was me she chose to share a blurred palette
seen from the car window. Azalea bushes strewn
with tiny skirts in temptress' colors,
little pink tongues lapping up the breeze …
becoming a preteen's riot, my mother's favorite.
As her shocking pink toenails worked the clutch,
she offered me a sip of her Gin Rickey through
a cellophane straw and tells me it was invented
by my late, great Uncle Rickey in Charlie's Tap
on the South Side of Chicago on VE Day in 1945.

She reaches across the seat to take it back
but I am busy sucking on the limes and biting ice cubes.

Blackberry Picking

Such a lot of bites and brambles
braved to taste
these hot, dark palpable beads,
veined and clotted purple.
Time remembered,
tongue and teeth
greeting with the heat of a dog
these hot-picked, high-noon treasures.

Aunt Kathleen scolds as she paints the red sores
with clear nail polish to suffocate
the chiggers buried beneath the bite marks
covering my arms and legs,
itching like anything.
Fiery parasites
lurk under the skin, spoilers
of stand-up berry picking in July.

Catfish Catch

Dried corn struck the pewter-colored surface.
The roiling pond
looking and sounding like hard rain
as in a frenzy the fingerlings fed.
Aunt Mae caught a two-foot
Catfish! complete with serious
whiskers and serious teeth.
The fish still fighting, Uncle
Jewel cut the line, drove
a nail through the cat's head
into the bark of a persimmon tree,
the body barely flapping now.
With a catfish-skinning tool,
he stripped its skin the way white bark
comes off a paper birch
of a piece. With pocket knife
he slit open its innards. Buried
in the dull gray lining were
ruby-colored, wet roe,
a handful of bright beads.
Jewel swore
and let the cluster of eggs
fall to the red clay at his feet.

Debutante on a Country Road

You, Apache Rain,
my prancing prince of plum blossoms,
high-stepping past the lowly honeysuckle,
neck arching as if on parade.
Just us two.
Tiger lilies, blackberry bushes,
tangled up snares of kudzu gone wild,
eruptions of yellow jackets.
You, quizzical
at creeping creatures,
rear up at the hollow echo
of concrete bridges.
You skittishly samba,
all legs, satiny ears,
your nostrils flaring at wild roses.

You take the bit in your teeth
as soon as we take that turn-around
towards home.
You take charge! You flat-out run!
Stretched out from hoof-to-hoof in midair,
like a drawing in an ancient cave.

I am praying I stay on board,
half-believing you are crazed enough
to run through barbed wire,
lose your footing
in your mad flight and kill us both—
almost home,
we are hurtling now,
you are maniacal,
not a horse but a dappled demon.
No one sees my fear.

The old women perspiring
in their garden rows think
I am crazy for speed,
as if I were asking for it.

That child is a holy terror.

Sweet Chariot

My cousin Tom, at age sixteen,
hit a bad stretch of road.
Tommy, who was thankfully alone,
was lit up with bubbly,
coming from a wedding party
where he was easily the Best Man.
Tom, who had never hit so much
as a turtle crossing the road,
who could charm the armor of an armadillo
and not take a feather off a crazed rooster
playing chicken across a dirt road,
this one man James gang of the highway
did the unthinkable,
fell asleep at the wheel.
The white Mercedes fishtailed into a cement bridge.
Tom was gone.

It was open casket.
The undertaker had been clever,
not enough.
"He had too many friends,"
said his many friends
as they closed the coffin.
Time was up.

A canopy of roses covered the casket
like the winning colt at the Derby
is blanketed in roses for finishing first.
I went out doors to have a smoke.
This cousin of mine could gentle any horse,
he was so still inside.

Cars, lined up like freight cars,
headlights on, Highway Patrol on hand
through a driving, drenching soaker.
In Mississippi, when the rain comes hard,
the red clay dirt turns into gumbo.
The hearse got balled up in the mud.
Car doors were flung open,
men and boys moved as one,
running in their church-going suits,
dress shoes engorged in the mud,
shouldering a burden,
they were aching to share.

St. Mick, First Crush

Once, you, a silver slip of a boy, not yet neon, were pouring gourds of water over me at a well on a beach in Morocco. Hashished I was into confusing your freckles with stars, myself so far gone I could only let you… Lucifer's hummingbird, stunning in purple gorget, shooting up skyrockets, pulsating throughout a less than eternal night. No masquerade there, Genius Boy! We were children then, still in possession of Desire, sharing a magnum of bubble-gum flavored Champagne, you offered me the South of France. We rocked and rolled and played about: you strutted tongue-in-cheek to the Devil's tattoo; I yelped with laughter, quick and high as a skimmer. You purveyor of Black Kif, but never a cloven-hoofed boy.

Yes! Glorious word! You, again, and I drank tea menthe, tasted the magical pipe…soon we were understanding Arabic, traveling the Venus Express, winking at the eyes of smoke trees. And the fishermen still put out at dawn.

Begging Pardon for Narcissus

I find I am always making excuses for Narcissus.
Haven't we all fallen in love with ourselves
At one time or another?

Isn't that after all the raison d'etre for mirrors?
Not to pluck our nostril hairs primarily?
But to admire the results?

Maybe he was an only child
Raised solely on the flickering still lifes of TV land?

Or one of Plato's shadowy shadows
Fattened on peeled grapes, pita and hummus
Before the word hug hit the lexicon?

Maybe he had just had corneal transplants
And his loveliness was the first sight of human-ness
He had ever beheld.

I admire him for drowning in beauty, even his own.
It is effortless to see ugliness mirrored everywhere one looks.

Summer of Love, July, 1969

Life was wet with promise.
There wasn't any real threat
in the word good-bye
and the Dock of the Bay
was never far away.

Men were walking on
that Mississippi moon,
that same night in July,
it was a clotted cream of a moon.
Sitting next to Rich
with the night wind
blowing in my face,
bugs and all,
as we pulled an all nighter
from the Chesapeake to the
heart of the Deep South,
I wanted to lick it all over.

When we went to the registrar in Canton,
Lightfoot Campbell put a pistol
on the counter when we signed the papers.
He had a surefire nose for Yankees.

We came out of the church in a hail of rice,
Slipped away to the Trace for a private embrace.

There, dressed as we were in full regalia,
we came across three codgers cooling off
in the shade of the everlasting pines.
Richie, drunk as a lord and twice
as goofy in his tux,
with me hovering at his side, dressed in a storm
of white and expectation,
called to them "Good Luck."

One of them, the color of eggplant,
spat tobacco on the ground,
raised his hand in return,
"Good luck to y'all."

Mississippi Born and Bred

The peepers are greenly piping
as we sleep and dream,
our arms flung every which way,
bodies curling around a warm,
safe memory of childhood birthday parties.

Both of us, only us,
wearing glasses,
lying shy, side by side,
on a picnic blanket.
Aunts and Uncles all around us
giving each other knowing looks.

Old enough now, here we lie,
our oh-so-separate thoughts arise.
Brown-limbed pages curling,
ink made invisible, ashes swirling
skyward from the bonfire
that is us.

A stinging thing with wings
caught in my hair as frantic as I am
until your hands release the struggling thing.

If not each other then who on earth
were we meant to love?

I Married Him Because He Asked Me

He is lying on the couch,
sleeping in his jeans by the fireplace,
empty quarts of Colt 45
lined up on the floor by his side.
Snoring with his mouth open,
he hugs himself in his sleep,
reaches for me with a little moan.
I am not there.
The dog lies beside him,
covered in dried mud.
The brass spittoon is wet,
stained with near misses of brown spit.
He has working hands,
honest hands that won't come clean,
even scrubbed with Lava and turpentine.

I protest nightly, exhausted, ridden into the dawn,
crying out loud like a frantic thrush caught inside the screen.
My outcry careens over acres of hay waiting to be baled,
over the hush of poplars, kudzu and bamboo,
disturbing only the standing bliss of horses and scattered cows.

My ruffle of poems, neatly stacked each evening
on the kitchen table, is set there beside cold,
congealed chicken and dumplings left from his supper.

His mama is kind to me, always,
even when once too many times
I appear at her house, unaware I am bleeding again.
This time the skirt she has made me is
soaked in a spread-eagled pattern of blood
as black as a nest of tarantulas.
She, schooled in country ways, lets me down easy.
"Between the two of you, it's never going to take."

The cool, pinkish light of dawn, finds me
boarding the train of my disappointments,
backpack in tow, it filled with a sheaf of lukewarm poetry.
I am heading North.

Heavenly Dust

He needed reminding to keep himself covered.
Dressed in a button-down cotton nightshirt,
I would find him lying as if in state in a bed piled high,
almost buried alive, in snowy comforters and pillowcases.
Honey-colored strips of tacky flypaper
dangled from the rafters in spirals clotted with black flies.
He never went hungry. His grandchildren brought him
meals on Sundays in glass dishes to eat during the week.
He talked food, sadly. "Every meal is cornmeal, grits,
fried everything, every kind of wet, fat-backed
soaked vegetable you can think of with tired,
made from a mix cornbread to mop it up with...

When I was a boy,
Sundays were a whole different story.
It was the white flour biscuits we lived for,
when white flour was so dear
we called it 'Heavenly Dust.'
He spoke about coming into
dinner at noon, from the fields,
when the heat made the air shimmer.
Blessing those hands that made this food,
thanking God in his mercy for what food there was.
He drifted. His sky blue, sightless eyes wandered.
He licked his lips, spittle seeping from the edges of his mouth.
He went silent remembering his mother's white flour biscuits.
I looked down at my hands folded in my lap.
He in his mid-nineties, myself, a child.

It took years and years and a stay in a convalescent home,
my own faculties in decline, waiting after every plate full
of the food I could barely touch with a fork,
for Juanita, my nurse, to bring me a coffee
rich with sugar, a dessert spoon and a small pitcher of hot milk...
It took all that for me to recall these visits vividly and fondly.

Unrelenting sun, unrelenting sweat,
the land cleared, the well dug,
the first to plant soybeans,
the last to get television.
The proud riot of grandchildren
and great grandchildren…
Hungry to inherit,
all of them missing the connection.
It is the taste of Heavenly Dust
on memory's tongue,
That redeems us
When the senses leave home.

Just Outside of Pickens

My favorite thing about Mississippi funerals was the food: red velvet cake, pineapple-upside-down cake, angel and devil's food and sock-it-to-me cakes and coconut pie, turnip green casseroles, green bean casseroles, tuna and potato chip casseroles, tomato gravy, black-eyed peas, butter beans, English and sugar peas and green snap beans all floating in a sea of fatback, fried chicken and fried catfish overflowing several platters, serving bowls brimful of fried okra, hush puppies, pear honey, competing versions of potato salad, three bean salad, macaroni salad and the most essential item-cornbread rich with bacon drippings, jalapeño and rat cheese cornbread and that sorry Martha White's white cornmeal, too sweet by half left stone cold and untouched, accompanied by pitchers and pitchers of sweetened and unsweetened tea, lemonade and Kool-Aid.

People driving by might wonder at the twenty or thirty odd, still shining pick-up trucks and family station wagons pulled up in the dirt turnaround in front of the old house, might think only poor folks have their washing machine on the front porch and the dogs keeping their cool underneath it. Visitors of mine from Millsap's college marveled at the primitive yellow spirals of flypaper hanging from the ceiling in every un-air-conditioned room, and were agog at the good little walk to the well and back for every drop used, remarking on the water as cool and sweet as water can be.

Perhaps this way of life was lacking in amenities, but by God, the McDaniels' owned the land on which they stood. It was welcomed when the children and their offspring bought or inherited more land to farm, to take that Four Cedars Road and line it on both sides with McDaniels' and sons of McDaniels' till it was known as McDaniels' Alley. That's how roads in the country get to be named. More acres, more farmland counted as good. Selling out was unforgivable, a treasonous betrayal. Only to be sold to another brother or brother-in-law, unthinkable to sell the land that had been cleared with a double-bitted axe, where the stands of pine had been left to anchor the red clay, the fields that McDaniels' and more McDaniels' and McDaniels' after that had followed a mule with a hand plow that turned the red clay furrows up into the light of day, had dug the well, kept the bees, been first in the county to raise Black Angus and dined on food so fresh it flipped in the pan. Amenities be damned.

The fat pine lighter kept the woodstoves lit in the cold weather, but one truly rotated one's backside, so cold and cruel the icy rains of winter. Housebound, the family made Christmas tree ornaments from pine cones, pecan shells and spiky hickory balls, and shot down mistletoe from the tops of trees to hang over every door lintel, read the family Bible every night and buried their own in a cemetery just down the road which was filled with McDaniels'. Walter, Walter, Walter Wayne, Walter Lloyd, Otha, Zebulon, Lloyd, Holly, Ruth, Ida Mae, Sydney and now the Phillips girl, Ruby, who died in childbirth, so pretty and so young, barely had time to become a married woman, still she produced a son. Some graves you just had to know who was buried there, the tombstones wrought illegible with time. Still the burial ground was kept up and washed with flowers, name or no name.

Crunching Gravel In the Trailer Park

Woke up to find I had locked my keys inside my car. Five cigarettes left and I hadn't paid my tab at the little store. Last night I had chauffeured a blind harp player to the Sunday night jam at the juke joint across the road, drinking sweet wine and drinking in Sam Myers' even sweeter blues. Sunday was the only night the races mixed there. God love them, the righteous were all in church.

Crunching gravel under foot, I go the long way around the circle of trailers, starting with the owned ones, headed towards the rentals.

The butcher's making soup again. He works the night shift at the Jitney-Jungle and has a yearning for the helpless, the delicious and the always on-the-brink-of-being-evicted divorcee in the down-at-the-heels section of the park. He calibrates if he feeds her, pays her utilities and rent, she will overcome her disgust for him and become his lover. "Hell, I'll marry her if it comes to that." No one likes him well enough to fill him in on what goes on while he is carving up sides of beef in the freezer with his arthritic hands.

Whoosh--Here comes Frankie Colombo in his Thunderbird—built back from nothing at all to a relic so American it belongs in the Smithsonian, and Frankie himself, not quite white enough, not quite dark enough, could be Prometheus, his smile bringing heat and light to a dark world—he grabs his lunch, kisses his mother on the cheek and tears up the gravel as he speeds out of the park.

Mama Rose, as she is known, has already started to make the meatballs and simmer her sauce for dinner. It is Monday. Tonight Frankie will eat and sleep at home.

Around the corner, the rentals begin, furnished, no AC, hotter than Hades, haul your own clinking trash bags to the dumpster, if you please. In the trailer park, on the shabby side, being put out on the street is not a figure of speech but a common occurrence.

Almost home, in the trailer parked next to mine, I hear more than I want to hear, see more than I want to see. A pitiful trailer, no curtains, nothing, just the dull, bass discord of a looming hulk named Popeye, between his child of a wife and the door. He has her cornered I can see, lumbering down the hall after her, complaining the coffee had soap in it, she shielding the infant in her arms--the only thing in her life that is hers.

Interrupted in his rage, he turns around fiercely towards a busy-body's furious chattering. Discovering it to be only a mockingbird having fun at his expense, spookily, he starts to laugh. After all, she will be here when he gets home. She has no place else to go.

He comes down the steps briskly, smiles when he sees me; he is ready to go to work. I think to myself I would rather die than ask this brute for anything, but I can't miss work again, they've already told me this is my last chance to even be late. He takes one of my coat hangers and jimmies the lock. Says I don't owe him anything. I am in my car and on my way to work in a flash, right behind him, spraying gravel every which way.

Beware the Thieves of Time

Mother's hydrangeas appear to be
heavily medicated,
their blossoms
so out of proportion to the rest of them.

They are to be found nodding out
in the gentlest of breezes,
their foam-white paleness, delicate
baby pinks and blues become
so valuable now,

thieves decapitate them,
fence them to black market florists who,
pretending not to know they are stolen property,
traffic in their exquisite fragility,
their short shelf life.

Mother, awakened by sinister
night noises on the carport,
waited up till dawn,
alone in the house,
afraid to make a sound,
rejoicing in the morning light to discover
it was only her old blue Buick that had disappeared
after midnight, in the wee hours.
The hydrangeas were safe.

The Road to Stockholm

I am standing in a glacier's bottom,
shaped like a kettle and
covered in brown leaves, mostly oak,
clotted with clean white clumps
of snow, somewhere in Sweden,
a country where I have never been.
At the brim, a roundabout,
one way must lead to Stockholm.
A woman dressed in a buckskin coat,
brightened with pink, yellow and blue
flowers of embroidery
gallops by on a good-sized pony.
This is the way to town, I am certain.
On foot it must be aways away.
A suggestion of stars trickles overhead,
enticing the twilight into a cobalt sky.
It is clear I will spend this night in the open,
walking this leaf-strewn path,
amongst these friendly trees,
shining patches of snow reflecting
the hungry moon, and no doubt
I will lie down in the night's commanding
cold, curled like a babe before birth,
saying the prayer he taught me as a child,
letting go of the light, welcoming the night.

Neither one of us ever took the time
to quarrel with god, though harsh,
and unrelenting god could be. My father,
speaking only once about Sweden, too dark,
he was glad to be free of the long, long nights.
Weighed down with my journey, I am
becoming a part of this winter,
without regret, without fear,
covering myself with leaves,
steadily, happily on my way
to a distant Stockholm. I have no need
to remember the pink stain a red mitten
leaves in a snowbank when retrieved,
or frigid fingers tangling laces after skating,
or father's sweater against my rosy face
flying into him in triumph some winter's afternoon.
It is enough to be here and to be his.

Musings and Remembrance

(For Arlene in memory of Dr. John F. Tannheimer)

Here comes the light step
The suggestion phrased as a question
Wisdom offered as possibility

Never as command
Behold the universe in all its wonder
The teacher upholds the beauty of life

The promise of diligence
The possibility of love, sister and brotherhood
Think of me when in doubt, he says,

For this father has no doubts
That life can be not only good
But a celebration.

Affection flows like a river
Smiling and patient and without ending.

Rocky Springs Farewell

We didn't really have a plan that afternoon.
We ended up at Rocky Springs.
A cold brook gives the place its name,
running clear along a stony, sandy bed,
so cold it makes the bones in your feet ache.
He held my hand so I wouldn't slip,
my protector and my guide.

When he was little he loved bananas,
couldn't quite get the word out.
I became Naner for always having
bananas in the kitchen for him.

Even though I was under strict orders
not to climb anything at all,
we climbed the hill where the young girls
are buried and it made him quiet.
Downed by Tuberculosis, Malaria,
redundant Diphtheria, sounding like Latin
names for flowering killers that might have
pursued Marie Antoinette if
her head had not already been spoken for.

He grew alarmed--alerted to danger
by an oncoming swarm of mosquitoes.
Thinking such desolate graves might be
contagious, we ran for the car. I turned my ankle.
Otha practically carrying me, we abandoned the
tombstones with their fading carved-in-stone dates.

His real send-off was to be with his friends that evening,
he fresh back from Ranger School, celebrating
an upcoming nine-month deployment out of Fort Bragg.

We stopped at Cock of the Walk in the late afternoon.
A fried-everything catfish house on the reservoir,
fish, french fries, hush puppies, onion rings,
    even pickles were fried.
The waiters would flip the cornbread in the air
from a cast iron skillet before they served you.
You could eat as much as you could hold for one price.
Otha loosened his belt a notch after pecan pie a la mode.

Otha, my one and only grandson,
toasted the Confederacy with Rolling Rock
after Rolling Rock.
"Forrest! Van Dorn! Pemberton! Lee!"
He was already talking too loudly,
never could drink worth his salt,
neither could his daddy.

It was Ulysses Grant
turned Jackson into Chimneyville,
had the fine ladies of Vicksburg dining on rats,

I reminded him. We salted our beers,
and it was the bubbles, not the South
that rose again, tickled our noses and
made us laugh. It took all I had,
letting him go like this behind
these non-stop let's pretends.

He, heading into a world
I could only imagine.
A living museum
from ancient times filled with
deafening noises, limbs lost,
killing blind and asking questions later,
disobeying every instinct, every grace
he'd been taught is manhood.
A world where the buddy next to him
becomes his last best hope for going home in one piece.

Family letters, heirlooms handed-down these many years,
map out this world. Letters kept, cherished,
in a small, teak casket inlaid with mother of pearl,
lined with scraps of rotten butternut fabric,
a dead watch and a missing fob, letters in a flowing hand
detailing a frantic cascade of perils and sacrifice.

Whatever happens to my Little One,
he is a soldier in this most recent,
futile, ill-conceived, misguided,
up-and-coming, never out-of-date
waste of lives and treasure,
conceived of and led by decent men doing
what their decent fathers did,
not knowing what else to do.

Whether it's black umbrellas
solemnly sprouting in the rain,
same as for my one and only Jewel,
now truly a jewel in the crown of the Lord,
or if my sweet grandbaby Otha
comes home with the breath still in him,
either way, I'm duty bound to wear
my smile like a flag.

Mona, 1945

Dad and Mona had married,
certain he was too old to be drafted.
But Roosevelt was calling,
desperate for soldiers.
The newly weds were
caught up in that deadly tide.

The war was just a parenthesis to him,
not to be confused with real life.
It unfolded with unimaginable bloodshed.
Every waking moment either one was
bored to death or in horror-driven overdrive,
staggering over stumps discarded,
men drowning in their own blood,
a waste, barbaric, not of his choosing.

When homecomings began many
of the ones who had seen combat
chose not to talk about the war,
buried their medals deep into the
top-dresser drawers of America.
Bronze Star, Purple Heart, changed nothing.
The dead were still dead.
Dad, finally discharged, his wounds tended to,
began his heart-healing journey home,
shy at the thought of happiness, long-delayed.

His Mona so good humored, he told me,
her eyes magnified behind gold-rimmed glasses,
periwinkle blue, crinkling at the corners
as if life was a parade of things to enjoy.
He remembered her in lilac;
they had read poetry to each other,
including Shakespeare's sonnets,
Donne's sonnets and her own.
They took turns winning at chess,
Mona embracing only him into her
circle of penetrating white light.

He, confident, life would begin again,
armed himself with hope and journeyed home.

Arriving at the gray, gabled boarding house,
where Mona's letters had brought him, he met
Pearl, her landlady, ankle deep in kindness.
She met him at the stairs and shushed him.
He found his Mona lying on a pyre of pillows,
hidden and slight under ironed cotton sheets pulled
clear up to her neck, in a Cloroxed
counterpane of covers.
She knew him, but couldn't speak,
herself a casualty of this Good War.
Tuberculosis claimed her, earned while
giving draftees at Fort Sheridan a magical gift,
teaching them to read.

He kept watch in his chair, counting at first the days,
then the hours, standing sentinel to each breath,
transfixed by the slight rise and fall of her breast.
There were moments he pressed his ear to her lips.
In this new terrain of grief
he needed God's help too much to curse Him.
Given no choice, somehow he bore it.

The landlady interrupted him,
bringing a cold washcloth to ease Mona's fever.

Go across the street and get yourself something to eat.

The late afternoon sun was
slanting against the window shade,
a rose-colored dusk creeping into the room,
dust motes fluttering. So he did.
He went across the street to a diner
made out of an old passenger train car
to grab a bite. While he was across the street
eating his sandwich, she died.

Casualties

I didn't buy a used car from him.
Still he offered to take me out to lunch.
The first thing I noticed was his bright pink rubber hand.
It was especially jarring as it didn't fit with the rest of him.
Neat as a pin. Flaming red hair cut short. Bright blue eyes.
Congenial nature. Suit and tie. Lunch led to drinks.
Makers Mark, Glenlivet, Bacardi 151--top shelf all the way.

We ended up on my screened-in back porch,
limp as laundry. He wooed me with woe, wooed me till
I was woozy with his tales of being a battlefield medic,
a maestro of morphine, a bringer of comfort
for the snowballs, those triaged in Viet Nam,
medivaced last, who didn't have a chance in hell.
It wasn't the screaming he told me, it was the whispers,
the scribbled, penciled promises, that went with the numbers
on the dog tags he had to scramble to keep track of:

If it is a girl, please name her Marie
After Mother, I know you two don't get along…

When I get home I'll make it up to you.
We'll get married, I promise you. A big wedding
Just like you want…

Please tell her I didn't mean to hit her.
I'd rather die than ever hurt her…

The morphine was scarce, the drops of alcohol precious.
The notebooks flapping in the wind from the helicopters'
rotor blades made his note-taking a blur,
the dying mens' requests got harder and harder to hear,
the letters got harder and harder to write.
He came home at the end of it all whipped
and drunk, guilty of the sin of despair.

He flew home to Texas. Honorably Discharged.
Drank all the way home and never came up for air.
In desperation, his daddy put him back to work in the
family business, a sausage factory. First day on the job,
Skipper, reeling and careening, got caught in
the grinder and lost his right hand.

I was tipping over, by story's end.
The last thing I remember, to my everlasting
shame, was getting sick and passing out.

He was gone when I came to.
The whole house stank of booze.
When I got it back right and smelling of Pinesol,
I knew my drinking days were done.

Years and years later, I wrote a poem about
that experience, thinking I understood him and his pain.
I read the poem, a version of this one, at an anti-war
reading, (it really doesn't matter which war) thinking
it was a long, long way from Galveston to Cambridge.
The poem mentioned Skipper, not by name, and
his ungainly pink rubber hand.

One of the listeners, a poet I respected,
a veteran, came up to me afterwards.
"You may not know this, but this man
you describe with the pink rubber hand
is famous, was a real hero in Viet Nam.
Not in the way you might think.

He's gone now, left a wife and daughter,
and not much else other than his buddies
and his good name, a handful of medals,
a drawer filled of medical bills the VA refused to pay.
They claimed his injury wasn't service connected.
Oh yes, and a couple of big wax egg cartons full of letters
from the families he wrote to, grateful for the fare thee wells
from their loved ones.

His wife, his high school sweetheart,
doesn't know what to do with the boxes.
She can't bear to throw them out.
They're all she has left.

It's the pink rubber hand that gives it away.
Next time you read this poem aloud,
and it's a good poem as far as it goes,
try leaving out the part about his hand.

For Him

She planted Tango geraniums
in the bed flanking the driveway
she had always wished was grander.
Still it circled the house, the house
she wished had pillars.

She coaxed shiny tulips
ordered from a catalogue to bloom
bright as fire trucks,
as well as curly coxcombs
and bloodied picadors
to lure the scarlet-crazed
hummingbirds with ruby throats
outside the picture window
where Dad parked himself
as the sun took its time
sinking and he read the
evening paper after work.

He hid behind his crossword puzzle
playing I Spy with the tiny birds
quick as locusts, wings timing
his countdown of memories even
during those last aching weeks
when his life was drawing to a close.

And so she tantalized him
with smiles
he could but nibble at,
like a sunfish
never quite taking the bait
hook, line and sinker.

She still had the power to raise
his wistful, crinkled gaze
that always seemed to question
how any woman as beautiful as she
could have ever ended up with any man
as ordinary as he?

His eyes remained
unchanged, adoring skies of blue,
while she held onto her tears
tighter than a miser's fist.

Cleanliness is Over-Rated

There is nothing funny about it.
This cleanliness next to Godliness business
drilled into you before you know what's hit you.
It starts with wiping mashed carrots off your chin
and ends with the white glove treatment
on the baseboards of your room.
So when the spring weather blew in on Friday
I vowed (what a perilous verb under any circumstance)
it was time for Spring Cleaning!

After all, one must consider it's Lent.
Time to sweep up the ashes of the deathly
New Year's Resolutions and ready myself for
Nature's bright yellow paintbrush, as she
conjures her wide swath of forsythia for my delight.

The fridge comes first, looking as if I had slaughtered a
small furry animal, perhaps a stray gerbil, beheaded by the
teeth of a pizza wheel, although as I scrub, I recall it was spilled
borscht, taking lots of hot water and elbow grease to scour
the icebox 'icebox white'.

This whole enterprise is so dreaded
I am ready to poke my head in the oven,
sadly it is an electric one. Again requiring
more muscle than I have, rubbing with a brush
to the point of seeing stars, pausing to rest and breathe,
then brushing again as I don't do fumes at least not
the abrasive, suck-out-your-lungs kind
with instructions on the bottle.
But then, there is a happy ending.

My house smells like pine trees,
like the Pinesol my mother always used
to clean her floors, and her mother as well.
That is the peace you cannot buy,
the peace that comes along with the clean house,
the house without a speck of dust, the house that shines,
the house that doesn't have a dust kitten hiding anywhere.

Oops! A stray Cheerio, under the counter. Yorick smiles.

Mother's Backbone

When Mother and I had the misfortune
to have no alternative but to leap to our deaths,
she blithely took my hand on the way down,
so we could go together, I thought.
As we sped downward,
she looked at me winningly
and said,
"Now don't forget to smile."

August, 1955
Historical Note

A 14-year-old African American young man,
barely a teen-ager, bright, beaming, full of life was
murdered by white men who were none of the above.
Down from Chicago in August, 1955,
visiting his Uncle Moses in a share-cropping town
in the Delta, a town called Money,
showing off for his country cousins,
or perhaps just in an effort to control
a speech impediment, Emmett Till was perceived as
whistling at a white woman in the town's
lone general store.
The woman's husband and brother-in-law,
in retaliation for this act, beat him to death.
They did it slowly. They bragged about having fun
beating this child to death. They gouged out his eye,
beat him so badly that in their trial, their defense
was that the body was so mutilated it could not be identified,
were found innocent, vindicated,
by a jury of their peers, cashed in and
sold their story to Look magazine,
bragging they were guilty.

The funeral director at Tutweiler,
did his best to prettify the corpse but could not.
The state of Mississippi tried to prevent
his mother from being permitted to open
the casket in Chicago, Illinois, but could not.
Jet magazine was there with its cameras and
published a photo of the young man's mutilated body.
His mother insisted on leaving the coffin
open at the funeral home for all to witness
what had happened to her baby.
50,000 walked past the body as it lay in state
It was called the nascent of the Civil Rights Movement.

Black Child's Summer Vacation
August, 1955, Sunflower County

When they met me at the station I couldn't understand my
Auntie Alice, Uncle Charlie and my cousin Flo at first,
their drawl was so thick. They teased me about my Yankee
accent, the grown-ups sweeping me up
in a torrent of embraces, strangers no more.

As for me and Flo, they called us the pick-up girls.
My stick-o-dynamite cousin, Flo, was big as a minute
at six, and me, down from Chicago on vacation,
big as a minute and a half at eight. A dark green
battered old Ford, took us everywhere we wanted to go.

Flo and I were in the bed of that truck
morning, noon and night. Wind blowing our braids,
red clay dusting our faces, our smiles steady.
Oh, how we loved the wind, the speed, the freedom,
holding on tight to the sides, sitting with our backs
close to the cab where Uncle Charlie could keep an eye on us.

Me and Flo.
We waved at everybody we passed
and everybody we passed waved at us.
Wherever one went, there went the other.
Whatever they were hauling in that truck,
flowers or fertilizer, watermelons or night crawlers,
Flo and I would ride.

 Flo and I were stretched out on taut, ironed sheets
fast asleep when I was awakened to voices in the kitchen.

"That boy had too much sense to whistle at a white woman.
He had a lisp. His S's might have sounded like a whistle."

Aunt Alice helped me get dressed without waking Flo.
She dressed me up in my Sunday School best,
my blue shirtwaist, white socks, and black patent leather shoes.
I knew I wasn't going to church in the middle of the night.

"They had already marked him. He talked like a Yankee.
14 years old. It was his accent. That whistle story was just an
excuse.

☞

What they did to that child even God cannot forgive."

Aunt Alice went to pack my pint-sized blue suitcase.
Uncle Charlie called me over. I stood up straight before him.

"If some white folks stop us do you know what to say?"
"Yes, Ma'am and Yes, Sir."
"That's right. If a white person talks to you remember
to look down at your shoes. Don't look at their face.
Can you do that for me, Baby Girl?"

Aunt Alice came out with my suitcase and a paper sack lunch.
I couldn't even speak, tears streaking.

"Really, Charlie, do you think that kind of talk is
    going to help this child now?
Are you trying to put the fear of God into her?" and then to me…
    "There's nothing wrong with you.
Your mama just wants you home, that's all it is."

The next thing that happened was Mr. Sam Jackson,
whom everyone seemed to turn to for advice
whether it was time to call the midwife or
when it was time to throw the first shovel
    full of dirt on the coffin,
drove up in the yard with his lights off.

Uncle Charlie had retreated to the front porch
where he sat with a shotgun across his lap.
Mr. Jackson came up, and took it from him.

"Leave it here. If we get stopped
it won't help any. Just make it worse."

So in a night with air as damp as the inside of an open grave,
in the same truck where Flo and I had flown so free,
now sat the three of us, me, this big-eyed eight-year-old
from the ins and outs of the South Side of Chicago,
anchored between two men strong as white oak trees,
the three of us bathing in the black of night,

blood smearing us as we slapped at mosquitoes,
listening to the bugle sounds of white mens' dogs
seeming to come from all around us.
We dodged the danger on those same back roads
Flo and I had ruled.

As we waited in the glow of the comforting
street lights of Jackson, trackside, for the Illinois Central
to light up the sky with bright beams of deliverance,
Uncle Charlie sat me down on my suitcase and made me
a picnic out of the sack of food Aunt Alice had fixed me.
As he calmed down, so did I.
And then with a quiet Halleluiah
as the train pulled into the station for a ten minute stop,
Mr. Sam Jackson leaned way down and took my hand,
as if overnight I had become a grown up,
and said to me in the kindest possible way,
"Now, Miss Ida Mae, You be sure to come back and see us now."
"Yes, Sir."

What the White Child Remembers
August 1955, Madison County

The Deep South contingent of Mother's family
picked me up in Canton, the county seat of Madison County.
I will always remember that first night.
Aunt Belle, Mother's baby sister, asked Uncle Earl if he wanted ice cream.
He said "Just a dab, please."
So she brought him a dish with just a dab, a teaspoon full
and everyone laughed. By the by,
it was hand-cranked ice cream full of cut-up peaches.
We were watching TV to see who would win
the Jitney Jungle contest for the free sewing machine giveaway.
I remember this because Aunt Kathleen actually won it.
What whooplah! Everyone said I brought good luck.
My slightly older cousin Bill took me for a ride on his chestnut gelding,
Dan, even though it was after dark. As we jumped a little crick I fell off
the backend.
Everyone teased me, "It helps to hold on."
In the morning Belle called out "Rise and Shine! Rise and shine!"

Bill's daddy let him drive a battered old
Chev-ro-lay pick-up truck, dark green,
to me the city child, golden, always splattered
with red Mississippi gumbo, always hauling something--
black-eyed peas, pecans, bushels and pecks, sweet feed,
hay bales, hound dogs, cases of cokes, orange and grape
soda pops and Dr. Peppers, odd paper sacks of clinking,
bootleg bottles from across the Pearl, bamboo poles, shotguns,
watermelons, night crawlers, martingales, road kill,
and Nigras, men and women both. These last rode in the truck bed.
The uncles said they smelled bad was why. I never smelled anything pecu-
liar.
Name your poison, work or play, those dark green Chevy trucks
had it going on those years; the joke about Fords was "Fix or repair daily."

One afternoon Bill and I were on our horses at the crossing in Canton
when the engineer of the Panama Limited waved at us and blew the horn.
My mare reared up and hit me in the nose and mouth.
Blood spouted everywhere. I could see Bill was shocked
and repulsed but he examined my wound anyway, and
told me it was going to be all right before he led me and
my normally docile horse home. I adored him.

In those old days, everyday was a promise kept.
Grinning at each other, bugs invading our smiles,
puppy love as deep and fresh as a watermelon cut,
one kiss that whole summer
when we barricaded ourselves in the saddle house.
Aunt Kathleen was at the door before we knew it,
so fast it made our heads spin. For our reward we got to clean
the rat-infested chicken house in our boots with hoses and shovels.
The baby rats were clean and pink, the size of a fingernail.
The grown-up rats had gleaming eyes that shown in the darkness,
baring their teeth, attempting to protect their young.

I was getting on the count-down side that August,
almost time to take the train back to Evanston and start school.
I didn't want to leave. And then something happened that
I thought for years afterwards was my fault.
It wasn't until I was grown that I put two and two together.
I got scolded only once the whole summer
but it stung like a hornet.
Uncle Will, the most gentle of all the uncles, a deacon at church,
a chaplain in the war, Bill's daddy, rarely raised his voice in anger
except one evening when we were sitting down to Chef Boyar-Dee,
butter beans and iced tea.
Aunt Kathleen asked if I wanted my tea sweetened or unsweetened.
 I remember saying in all innocence, "I don't care."
Uncle Will went off like a bomb.

"Don't you ever let me hear you say
'I don't care' again, Young Lady!
Say 'I don't mind' all you like,
but don't you ever let me hear
you say the words, I don't care."

Then instead of holding hands and saying grace as always he said,
"What kind of world are you children going to grow up in?"
He walked out the back door letting it slam, without touching his supper.

Aunt Kathleen, not herself, didn't say a word and filled our plates.

"Free the Whitfield 3000"

Whitfield State Hospital, Pearl, Mississippi 1985

Rain erases
the evidence of my tears
sending me downstream too fast.
People see my open mouth
gasping for air, my bones trying to balance,
trying to land on my feet and
not landing at all.
I busy myself denying that I am different
until the dark ravens, the floaters of madness,
(the be all and end all of being locked up)
make carrion of my hopes, my loves, my me.
Am I totally lost? Is this sand? Or sugar?
Is the grass growing or
is it pulsing skyward in a vertical tide?
Is this love or heavy breathing?
My eye sockets are cracked and dry
as a dried-up lakebed.
My vision is stifled by nurses in cages,
windows opaque with grime.
Industrial weight screens
protect the world from me.

I see soybean fields running in
place, straight lines boxing in
my memory along with
endless rows of cotton bolls
cut with a famous two-lane highway
as it scolds its way north through
Greenville, Cleveland, Carthage
and Tunica.

Confined in a cage in the city of Pearl,
I hold my breath an impossibly long time,
trying to die. Failing and surrendering,
I slowly and completely exhale.
It is the Mississippi Delta flying by me
outside the car window.
Mythical, merciless, haunting and my own.

There the eye is free to travel as far as it can see.
Here I am locked up inside a building...
no sky, no dawn nor dusk, nor sweep of eye.
Are you coming? Are you here yet?
My boundaries are the peeling paint
on the green wall of the day room,
my bounty, the plastic chartreuse plates
of the hospital cafeteria
filled with gritty grits and limp turnip greens.
My prize, vanilla ice cream in a blue and white
Dixie cup with a wooden spoon.
The toilets in the locked unit are
cleverly and spitefully
always without toilet paper.
The wire gates are kept locked,
clanging only for passage to the shrink's office
or to the showers at dawn.
My naked body is hosed down after the soap up
by bored women in state hospital uniforms.
The smells of nature being human nature--
are sweat, feces, urine standing in the bowl.
We, the outlaws and oddballs,
stalk the corridors shouting and wailing,
struggling for definition, already smelling of rot,
truly left for dead.

The bright spots of the day,
a cup of Sanka and graham crackers
at snack time,
an hourly smoke, a haze of hope.
Day upon day, I call your name
believing that you will hear me and come,
that you still want me and will show up,
believing against all evidence,
that I've got a friend and that friend is you.
Where and who am I without your music?
Where am I now without your compass?
I am refusing, straightjacket or not,
to love the one I'm with.

It gets worse.
This morning—no breakfast.
They lie me down like a horse that refuses to eat,
put a bit in my mouth, a rubber thing to bite on,
a rough and ready pacifier so my teeth
don't grind themselves away.
They strap me down
in four point restraints
so I won't break my limbs
thrashing around when they apply
the electric shock.

They think I am too lazy to kill
my only self
and so to save me the trouble
they will do it for me.
A deep breath and a quick trip
behind the black velvet curtain,
and yet the diamonds
they so coveted have disappeared,
flown away, migrated to another sphere,
stolen from my mind's eye, blank now,
leaving only moth holes behind.

Without consequences to them
the damage was done by thieves
in white coats in broad daylight.

Their task to erase a person's memory,
palpitating without the requisite gloves
the only possession that cannot be stolen.
Their tomfoolery doesn't work.
It seems memory is not the only
light that binds.
Love is love. Damn the details.
Operation Love Another has failed.

When I re-enter my sarcophagus of a being
there remains only you.
The name of you shouting out from me
up and down the hallways,
all 92 pounds of me…
rolling my own smokes,
trying to get you on a telephone
I can no longer figure out how to operate.
Crying out my rage and grief
at the black phone receiver.
Where are you?
Where am I without you?

They give up trying to heal me
if that is what they were trying to do.
After Mother's pleading,
they released me, sent me home
with a prescription guaranteed
to neuter and to neutralize.
They promise me if I take my medicine
I won't feel anything at all.
No pain, they promise, no pleasure.
If pleasure is the absence of pain,
then pain must be the absence of pleasure,
and the numbness
I am left with in this equation amounts only
to a walking, talking death.

Mother and I flushed the thorazine
and she put me on a train at Meridian.
The train was going north towards
Boston, the Cradle of Liberty.
She held me tight as we waited.
I held her back…on my way
to a realm where I hoped freedom
was more than talked about.

Pinehaven

I lost my appetite.
High as a kite I was,
a side effect of not eating.
Thoughts coming and going
like birds at dusk or at dawn.
Neurons really.
There is no
mercy of the bored,
upon whom I depend
at Pinehaven,
the nursing home I inhabit
in direct contradiction to my
over-my-dead-body instructions.
All of a sudden I see that
daughter of mine
leaning over my bed,
her face in my face,
God love her.
Do you know where you are?
I notice I am not at Pinehaven,
I am in a hospital.
They want to try a feeding tube.
We should try it, don't you think?
Isn't that what we've always
been about? Trying our best?
They never gave me food
again at Pinehaven.
Instead they gave the order
nothing by mouth.
Lickety-split, in half the time,
they fed the hole in my stomach.

Muscles atrophy from not chewing.
Muscles atrophy from not speaking.
I ripped out the feeding tube.
My Judas daughter with the big job
flew in from Gay Paree
to sign the consent forms
to reinsert the feeding tube.
Once again she quailed
in the face of the white-coated
saleswomen of longevity.
Miss High Muckety Muck
who cost me and her father
a fortune to educate went limp
before their guilt-soaked incantations.

They undo the drip from
the back of my hand.
The tube is in place.
My daughter wants to know,
What are those for?
"These are two-point restraints
to be certain she won't pull out
the feeding tube again."
It's lunchtime.
They don't bring me a tray.
The nurse pulls back the blanket.

My child watches as
the nurse pours.
My intestines rebel,
the fluids overspill.
I aspirate this slimy
cream of mush.
I am blue in the face
choking on my vomit.
My girl
sees them call the code,
sees them rush into the room,
sees them resuscitate me,
sees how when I am revived
I try to bite the staff that has
brought me back to life.

So this child of mine
takes off without a word,
reappears with a plastic
hospital-issue pitcher of ice,
unbuckles the leather

restraints on my wrists
already starting to chafe
the skin raw where the
drip had been.
She pulls back the vomit-stained blanket
tearing the already ragged skin
as little as possible,
(her major was Art Restoration)
worries free the feeding tube,
tucks me in again,
and with crushed ice starts mopping
my firecracker-hot face to some tune…
I cannot remember the words.

Bucket Head

I

She moved into the other half of the duplex
I owned on the colored side as it was called then
of Fortification Street-
where Grant had broken through the Confederate lines
and turned Jackson, Mississippi,
into Chimneyville.

With her she brought
all of two trash bags.
Her hair looked like the
nest of a magpie
done up in platinum blonde.
But she showed up alone,
and she was
Showing.
I couldn't bring myself
to turn her away.

She kept to herself.
Got up in the morning,
went somewhere,
dressed neatly under that banshee hair-don't.
Never brought groceries home.
Her car
parked in the side lot
was littered with soda cans and
fast food wrappers.

She carried brown paper bags into the house
clinking like liquor bottles.
Never brought any out.
One day she came over,
knocked at my door,
classifieds in hand.

A German shepherd?
A female spayed?
Would it be okay?

The poor, pitiful thing.
What would a good shampooing and brushing do?
A trip to the beauty shop was what she needed,
a spot of lipstick,
not a dog.

All alone she was,
not even a pretend ring.
Her legs and arms stick thin,
I said yes,
she would have to keep it outside.

She brought the dog home
in early June--
the sorriest looking dog I had ever seen.

She's been on a chain her whole life.
She apologized for the dog, now
skulking low to the ground,
head turned sideways,
anticipating a blow…
She dragged it up the steps.
I am going to call her Tess.

"What was her name before?"
She didn't have one.
She was just chained up outside in their back yard.
They just wanted her gone.
I'll tie her up in the yard.
she said obligingly.

"It appears to me she's done enough
time at the end of a chain."
My tenant gave me a grateful smile before
hauling the dog into her half of the duplex.

Moments later they reappeared,
Tess bravely adorned in red leash and collar,
her mistress in a white sunhat pulled over
that hair's nest, a great improvement.
But Tess didn't know how to walk on a leash.
To walk her was hard, sweaty work for the girl.

On one of those walks, up towards
the white side of busy Fortification,
stopping to buy a soda,
or sitting on someone's steps to cool off,
he must have spotted her
taking a breather along East Fortification Street.

It was hot as Hades,
almost the fourth of July,
close enough so fireworks could be heard
off and on in the neighborhood.
My main concern was keeping cool.
I turned the AC on in the bedroom
and put on my housecoat.
It was time for The Price Is Right.

And then I heard shots fired.
Not cherry bombs,
Gun shots.
The shots were
coming from my front door,
then into the living room.
I am no fool.
I keep a loaded handgun in my nightstand.
My brother's doing.

So I snatched up my gun and started shooting back.
The shooter hadn't figured that the person,
the woman, who lived there would have a gun and
be able to shoot back,
defend herself.
Like the coward he was,
he ran.

I got a good look at him.
He was white and wore a Bull Durham cap.
I knew right away he had miscalculated
which side of the duplex she lived in.
Tess was moaning a low feral moan
through the screen door.
Her mistress,
whatever her name was,
stood silent and completely still.

She knew she had to go.
Like a marionette
she headed to her car empty-handed,
not even a toothbrush.

I went to my Bible and gave her
four one hundred dollar bills and four twenties.
"Don't worry about the damn dog;
I will take care of Tess."
I cannot tell when white folks are pale or just white.
She looked gray.
Grabbed my hand and kissed it,
held it to her cheek,
started her car and took off.

When the rent was due
and she hadn't contacted me,
I went inside for the first time.
It was neat and clean and empty.
She had been sleeping
on a pile of neatly folded blankets and clothes.

What I had heard clinking were pieces of pottery,
not like any pottery I'd ever seen.
Glistening and strange,
more varieties than a body could dream up
or want or wish for.
Some I could figure out a use for,
some I couldn't.

I started out with good intentions.
I would pick up some corn-husk tamales
on Farish Street and walk the dog at the same time.
There I was dragging Tess by her leash and of a sudden
I jerked her up to where I was standing.

I took the leash off.
Go on now, Tess.
Time to find another friend.
Tess wouldn't budge,
wouldn't even look at me.

So I gave her a shove.
She still cowered beside me.
I kicked in her direction,
raised my voice.
Still she wouldn't move.
I hollered at her and
tried to hit her with my open hand,
then with the leash.
Kicked at her again
and missed again.
Raised my hand to her,
off she ran.

II

Again it's early summer time,
this day is a scorcher.
I have plugged my fan in,
set it outside to blow on me
as I sit on the porch.
Even so my scalp is wet with sweat.
I am still working nights,
going to the same job,
still not part of a couple. I was
sitting and reading the Clarion Ledger,
locally known as the Carrion Dredger.

On the front page,
a photo of a dog,
a shepherd with a plastic bucket over its head
held by two
police officers caught in the act
of removing the bucket.

The cutline reads:

This dog nicknamed Bucket Head
By the children in this Jackson neighborhood
Has eluded capture for many months
Surviving only by the kindness of families
Who over the winter put out food for her.

Not So Old Married Couple

I am so happy
to be here with you
in a world of our own making,
wrapped in the comfort of earth and sky.
Should I fail to look both ways
and begin to cross the street
into traffic while lost in thought,
you will take me by the hand,
or say my name,
and set me on course again.
There will be
no need for embarrassment, or hurt feelings,
because if I forget, you will remind me
I am perfect in every way.
Which is what lovers do.
My love does, and that is you.

Tap Water Please

Sunday evening I was
crossing the bridge from
Boston into Cambridge.
Dusk had colored
the sky mauve
over the bland vanilla
frappe of the frozen Charles.
Something startled me.
I couldn't shake it off.
I stopped walking,
relinquished my backpack.
Snow had been falling
lightly since Friday and
I was crossing into
Cambridegeport,
as I did every Sunday
evening, heading home from
my home away from home.
I paused, shocked at the pain,
sat on the steps at M.I.T.,
holding myself in my arms,
not wanting to make a fuss.
This was Cambridge, after all.
I knew what to do.
I took an aspirin,
swallowing it with spit.
Didn't call anyone.
Found my way home.
No regrets.
Not much of a surprise.
Truly. It runs in families.
Still, when the moon
wouldn't quit that night
and the orange glow of
Boston's light pollution
made falling asleep unlikely,
I took my last
pack of Camels
and threw it off the balcony
like a little girl throws a nickel
into a fountain for good luck.

Dream Come True

Time impales me
on the tip
of my senses
as no sunset,
nor constant star
ever could.
When I die
I'm going to live
on the other side
of your shy eyes.

Linda Larson

Linda Larson was born and educated in the Midwest and spent childhood vacations and more than a decade of her adult life in Madison County, Mississippi. She attended Lawrence University in Appleton, Wisconsin, and graduated with a Masters of Arts from the Writing Seminars at Johns Hopkins University in 1970. While in Mississippi, she worked as a feature writer for The Capitol Reporter and The Jackson Advocate. Larson relocated to the Boston/ Cambridge area where she has lived and worked for the past twenty-five years.

For five years she served as editor of and contributor to Spare Change News, a homeless newspaper based in Cambridge. In 2007, she published her first book of poetry, Washing the Stones, Ibbetson Press.

www.ingramcontent.com/pod-product-compliance
Lightning Source LLC
Chambersburg PA
CBHW021912040426

42447CB00007B/822